A WOMAN'S NOTEBOOK

edited by Elaine Goldman Gill
designed by AnneMarie Arnold

The Crossing Press • Freedom, CA 95019

Never let go of that fiery sadness called desire.
—Patti Smith

Nature is the teacher, revealing the mysteries of life. Nature is not a power to be harnessed or overcome.

—Diane Mariechild

The fantastic and unexpected, the ever-changing
and renewing, is nowhere so exemplified as in
real life itself.

—Berenice Abbott

Male and female are really two cultures and their life experiences are utterly different.
—Kate Millett

Women have served all these centuries as look-
ing-glasses possessing the magic and delicious
power of reflecting the figure of man at twice its
natural size.

—Virginia Woolf

If you don't like what you were as a child, you still have to accept that child as part of you, the imaginative, frightened, creative soul.
—Elaine Goldman Gill

I've been through it all, baby. I'm Mother Courage.

—Elizabeth Taylor

Like woman herself, the family appears as a natural object, but is actually a cultural creation.
—Juliet Mitchell

Macho does not prove mucho.

—Zsa Zsa Gabor

If God is male, then the male is God.
       —Mary Daly

Reality is something you rise above.
—Liza Minnelli

A photograph is a secret about a secret. The more
it tells you, the less you know.

—Diane Arbus

I like fame, but don't like and am no good at its requirements.

—Lillian Hellman

I've never cared what others thought of me.
With me it was always—just me.

—Ethel Waters

It gave me great pleasure to think I could take wood, make it good, and people like Rockefeller buy it with paper money.

—Louise Nevelson

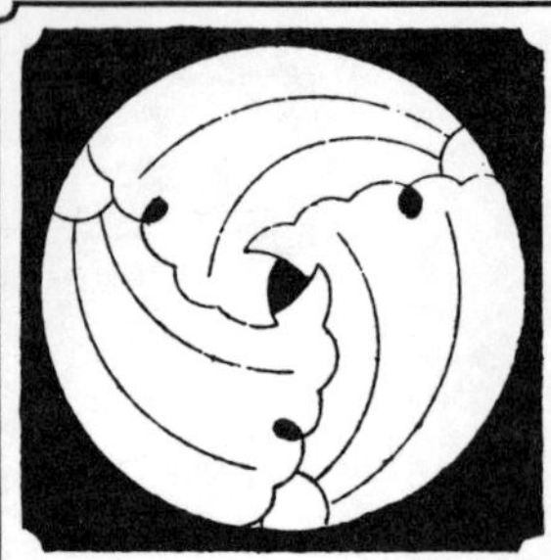

Some women want to be gripped inside their clothes. Never. I want women to enter my dresses and to hell with everything else.
—Coco Chanel

Not many jobs require a penis or a vagina... All jobs should remain open to anyone.
—Gloria Steinem

Sooner or later I'm going to die, but I'm not going to retire.

—Margaret Mead

Woman will not be free as long as walking down the street, with eyes straight ahead, stomach contracted, is like running the gauntlet.

—Ann Sheldon

If men could get pregnant, abortion would be a sacrament.

—Florynce Kennedy

For us, the superwoman who knits marriage, career, and motherhood into a satisfying life without dropping a stitch is as oppressive as the airbrushed Bunny in the Playboy centerfold.
—Sylvia Rabiner

The more successful you get, the more you tend to intimidate the men around you whom you may want to get next to.

—Bonnie Raitt

The individual artist ethic has been very destruc-
tive to women, because when men are alone,
they aren't really alone—they are alone in their
studios supported by systems. But women are
really alone, without any system, and that is not
just alone—that is isolated and powerless.
—Judy Chicago

I saw that nothing was permanent. You don't want to possess anything that is dear to you because you might lose it.

—Yoko Ono

Be very romantic, but keep the real estate in
your own name.

—Erica Jong

Death is like putting away your winter coat when Spring comes.

—Elisabeth Kubler-Ross

To get it right, be born with luck or else make it.
Never give up.

—Ruth Gordon

I am a woman meant for a man, but I never found a man who could compete.

—Bette Davis

The breakers of hearts, the queens of romance, the goddesses of a thousand devotees, have not been cooks.

—Charlotte Perkins Gilman

Reality is something you rise above. Men's favorite method of arguing against women is to deny their statements of fact.

—Christabel Pankhurst.

Of my two "handicaps," being female put many
more obstacles in my path than being black.
—Shirley Chisholm

The sucess of the feminine-hygiene spray provides a fascinating paradox in that its manufacturers have taken advantage of the sexual revolution to sell something that conveys an implicit message that sex—in the natural state—at least—is dirty and smelly.

—Nora Ephron

There is no deoderant like success.
                    —Elizabeth Taylor

Black women have been doubly oppressed. White women have their problems. They're interviewed for secretarial instead of the executive thing. But we're interviewed for mopping floors.

—Margaret Wright

I never loved another person the way I loved myself.

—Mae West

Did anyone ever tell Toscanini or Bach that
he had to choose between music and family,
between art and a normal life?
—Elisabeth Mann Borgese

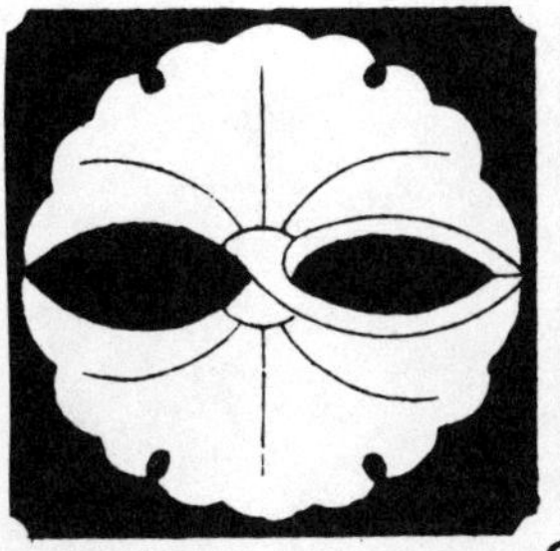

Sometimes I worry about being a success in a mediocre world.

—Lily Tomlin

I can always be distracted by love, but eventually
I get horny for my creativity.

—Gilda Radner

The biggest sin is sitting on your ass.
—Florynce Kennedy

Let it all hang out. Let it seem witchy, catty, dykey, frustrated, crazy... nutty, ridiculous, bitter, embarrassing, man-hating, libelous, pure, unfair, envious, intuitive, low-down, stupid, petty, liberating. We are the women that men have warned us about.

—Robin Morgan

We will have equality when a female schlemiel
moves ahead as fast as a male schlemiel.
                                        —Estelle Ramey

Because I am I, and odd piece of Egotism who could not make the riffle of living according to the precepts and standards society demands of itself, I find myself locked up with others of my kind in a "hospital" for the insane. There is nothing wrong with me—except I was born at least two thousand years too late. Ladies of Amazonian proportions and Beserker propensities have passed quite out of vogue and have no place in this too damned civilized world.

—Lara Jefferson

Everybody's mother still cares.

—Lillian Hellman

Nobody outside of a baby carriage or a judge's chamber can believe in an unprejudiced point of view.

—Lillian Hellman

The truth is that Aid to Families with Dependent Children is like a super-sexist marriage. You trade in a man for *the* man. But you can't divorce him if he treats you bad. He can divorce you, of course, cut you off anytime he wants. But in that case, *he* keeps the kids.

—Johnnie Tillmon

Revolution is the festival of the oppressed.
—Germaine Greer

If love is the answer, could you rephrase the question?

—Lily Tomlin

I was surprised, at quite a late age, to find I had a pretty strong movie going on in my head—for me, it was the delicious anticipation of a frightful accident: me involved in a bloodly accident, me lying at the bottom of a flight of stairs. There's no way of getting rid of such a movie. You've got to live with it, but you can recognize the old movie and laugh at it.

—Elaine Goldman Gill

Consciousness-raising is speaking the un-
spoken.

—Juliet Mitchell

It's not the men in my life that counts
—it's the life in my men.

—Mae West

If anyone should ask a Negro woman what is her
greatest achievement, her honest answer would
be, "I survived."

—Pauli Murray

I'm not radical—I'm just aware. I've come a long way, baby.

—Billie Jean King

Marriage should be a combining of two whole, independent existences, not a retreat, an annexation, a flight, a remedy.

—Simone de Beauvoir

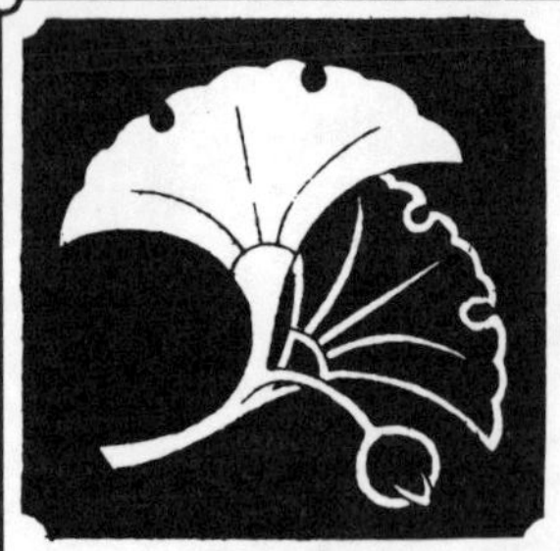

If my business was legitimate, I would deduct a substantial percentage for depreciation of my body.

—Xaviera Hollander

I asked a friend, a vice-president at a big corpo-
ration, how much of her woman energy she had
to thrust down, to hide. I was astonished when
she said 80%. What a waste! No wonder women
become entrepreneurs.

—Elaine Goldman Gill

If there is one feeling, above all others, I would implant in a girl, it is self-reliance.

—Virginia Penny

If you're any one of these things—poor, black, female, middle-aged, on welfare—you count less as a human being. If you're all of these things, you don't count at all.

—Johnnie Tillman

Women have always been healers. They were the unlicensed doctors and anatomists of Western history. They were abortionists, nurses and counsellors. They were pharmacists, cultivating healing herbs and exchanging the secrets of their uses. They were midwives, travelling from home to home and village to village. They were called "wise women" by the people—witches or charlatans by the authorities.

—Barbara Ehrenreich and Deirdre English

The trouble with the rat race is that, even if you win, you're still a rat.

—Lily Tomlin

Call on God, my dear. She will help you.
—O. H. Belmont

Surely to primitive people the ability to give birth must have seemed a far greater miracle than the mere possession of am observable, push-me, pull-me, shrink-and-grow penis, however interesting and even worthwhile this organ may be.

—Barbara Seaman

Be good to yourself.